Paul Strathern

DESCARTES
(1596–1650)
in 90 minutes

Constable · London

First published in Great Britain 1996
by Constable and Company Limited
3 The Lanchesters, 162 Fulham Palace Road
London W6 9ER
Copyright © Paul Strathern 1996
The right of Paul Strathern to be identified as author
of this work has been asserted by him
in accordance with the Copyright,
Designs and Patents Act 1988
ISBN 0 09 475950 2
Set in Linotron Sabon by
Rowland Phototypesetting Ltd,
Bury St Edmunds, Suffolk
Printed in Great Britain by
St Edmundsbury Press Ltd,
Bury St Edmunds, Suffolk

A CIP catalogue record of this book
is available from the British Library

All translations are by the author.

DESCARTES IN 90 MINUTES

Contents

Introduction and background to his ideas

By the end of the sixteenth century philosophy had stopped. It was Descartes who started it up again.

Philosophy had begun for the first time in the sixth century BC in Ancient Greece. Two centuries later it entered a golden era with the advent of Socrates, then Plato and Aristotle. After this, for nearly two thousand years, nothing happened. Nothing original that is.

Of course, several distinguished philosophers appeared during this period. The third-century Alexandrian Plotinus refined Plato's philosophy, in the process creating Neoplatonism. St Augustine of Hippo then refined Neoplatonism to the point where it was acceptable to Christian theology. The Islamic scholar Averroes refined parts of Aristotle's philosophy, and Thomas Aquinas in turn rendered these acceptable to Christian theology. All four of these disparate figures advanced the course of philosophy, but not one of them produced an entirely new philosophy of his own. Their work was essentially exegesis, commentary and elaboration of the philosophy of Plato and Aristotle. In this way, these two pagan philosophers (and their pagan philosophies) became pillars of the Christian Church. This intellectual conjuring trick was the main foundation of Scholasticism, the name given to philosophical activity during the Middle Ages. Scholasticism was the philosophy of the Church, and prided itself on its lack of originality. New philosophical ideas only resulted in heresy, the Inquisition and burning at the stake. The ideas of Plato and Aristotle gradually became buried beneath layers of theologically correct Christian commentary, and philosophy dried up.

By the mid fifteenth century this moribund stage had been reached in almost all fields of intellectual endeavour. The Church reigned supreme throughout the medieval world. But already the first cracks were beginning to appear in this vast edifice of intellectual certainty. Ironically, the main source of these cracks was the very classical world which had produced Plato and Aristotle. Much learning that had been lost or forgotten during the Dark Ages now began coming to light, inspiring a renaissance (or re-birth) of human knowledge.

The Renaissance brought with it a new humanistic outlook. This was followed by the Reformation, which ended the hegemony of the Church. Yet over a hundred years after these developments had transformed Europe, philosophy still remained stuck in the bog of Scholasticism. This only came to an end with the arrival of Descartes, who produced a philosophy fit for the new era. In no time this spread through Europe, and even achieved the ultimate accolade of being named after its founder: Cartesianism.

Life and work

Descartes never did a stroke of useful work in his life. At various times he described himself as a soldier, a mathematician, a thinker and a gentleman. The latter comes closer to describing his attitude to life, as well as his social status. His youthful inclination to a life of leisurely ease soon settled into a routine. He lived on his private income, rose at noon, and travelled a bit when he felt like it. And that was it. No dramas, no wives, no great public success (or failure). Yet Descartes was indisputably the most original philosopher to appear in the fifteen centuries following the death of Aristotle.

René Descartes was born on 31 March 1596 at the small town of la Haye, some thirty miles south of Tours. This spot has now been renamed Descartes, and if you visit it you can still see the house where he was born, as well as the twelfth-century church of St Georges where he was baptized.

René was the fourth child, and his mother was to die in childbirth the following year. His father Joachim was a judge in the High Court of Brittany. This met at Rennes, 140 miles away, which meant that Joachim was at home for less than half the year. He soon remarried, and René was brought up in the house of a grandmother. Here his main attachment was to his nurse, for whom he retained the fondest regard. He was to pay for her upkeep until the day she died.

Descartes spent a solitary childhood, this isolation accentuated by his sickly nature, and he quickly learned to do without company. From his early years he is known to have been introspective and reserved: a wan-faced child with thick curly black hair and large shadow-ringed eyes, wandering through the orchard in his black coat and knee breeches, a black wide-brimmed hat on his head and a long woollen scarf wound around his neck.

At the age of eight Descartes was sent as a boarder to the Jesuit College which had recently opened in la Flèche. This school was intended for the education of the local gentry, who prior to this had often dispensed with such matters in favour of hunting, hawking and half-hearted home homiletics. The rector of the college was a friend of the Descartes family, so the frail young René was given a room of his own and allowed to get up when he pleased. As with most who are permitted such a privilege, this meant that Descartes rose around noon – a habit he strictly adhered to for the rest of his life. Whilst the other pupils were being brow-beaten by vicious and conceited Jesuits fiendishly versed in the intricacies of Scholasticism, the intelligent young Descartes was thus able to absorb his learning in a more relaxed atmosphere, rising in time for luncheon – followed by the riding, fencing and flute-playing lessons which occupied the afternoon. By the time he came to leave, it was apparent that Descartes had learned far more than anyone else in the school, and his health appears to have completely recovered (apart from a lingering hypochondria, which he carefully nursed throughout his remarkably healthy life).

Yet despite carrying off all the prizes, Descartes retained a deep ambivalence towards his education. It seemed to him to be largely rubbish: rehashed Aristotle encrusted with centuries of interpretations, the stifling theology of Aquinas which had answers for everything but answered nothing – a morass of metaphysics. Nothing that he learned appeared to have any certainty whatsoever, apart from mathematics. And in a life devoid of the certainties of home, family and meaningful social contact, Descartes craved for certainty in the only realm he felt at home: the intellect. He left school disappointed. Like Socrates before him, he was convinced he knew nothing. Even mathematics was only capable of providing impersonal certainty. The only other certainty he knew was God.

When Descartes left la Flèche at sixteen, his father sent him to study law at the University of Poitiers. Joachim Descartes intended that René should take up a respected post in the legal profession, just as his elder brother had done. In those days such posts were filled largely through nepotism – a system which succeeded in producing approximately the same percentage of ludicrous and inadequate judges as the system in use today. But after spending two years taking a law degree Descartes decided that he'd had enough of the law. By this stage he had come into possession of a number of small rural properties, inherited from his mother. These gave him a modest income – enough to live as he pleased. So he set off for Paris 'to pursue his thoughts'. Judge Joachim was not pleased. The Descartes were gentlemen – they weren't expected to spend their time thinking. But there was nothing he could do about it: his son was now a free man.

After two years Descartes became tired of his well-heeled bachelor existence in Paris. Despite devoting himself to a wide range of studies, and composing a number of rather dilettantish treatises, he was becoming increasingly involved in the social life of the capital, which he found utterly tedious. This was no reflection on fashionable Parisian society of the period. Descartes appears to have found all social life tedious, and would probably not have appreciated how uniquely tedious this particular society was. Descartes withdrew to a quiet address in the Faubourg St Germain, where nobody but nobody went visiting anybody who was anybody. Here he lived in seclusion and continued to pursue his thoughts in peace.

This was to be Descartes' favoured mode of existence throughout the rest of is life. Yet

after settling down for a few months, he suddenly upped sticks. Descartes seems to have
been driven by two finely balanced obsessions:
solitude and travel. Never having felt close to
his fellow men, he had no wish to live in their
company. And never having had a real home,
he felt no desire to create one for himself. He
was to remain forever restless and solitary.

This makes Descartes' next decision seem
all the more extraordinary. He decided to join
the army. In 1618 he went to Holland and
signed on as an unpaid officer in the army of
the Prince of Orange. The Protestant army of
the Prince of Orange was preparing to
defend the United Provinces of the Netherlands against the Catholic Spanish, who
wanted to retake their former colony. So what
did the Dutch make of this aloof Catholic
gentleman with no military experience, who
professed to have done a bit of fencing and
riding at school? It's difficult to judge. At the
time Descartes spoke no Dutch, and stuck res-

olutely to his routine of rising at noon. Perhaps they just didn't notice him, as he sat in his tent composing a treatise on music or some such. (Nowadays he would presumably be accused of being a spy; but in those days the military appear to have correctly gauged the importance of spies, and been willing to sign on any recruits regardless of nationality, allegiance or even willingness to participate in military routine.)

We do know that Descartes found himself bored by life in the army; there was 'too much idleness and dissipation', in his view. Does this mean there were officers who got up even later than he did? If the Spanish had launched a surprise morning attack, it looks as if they might have encountered some stiff opposition from a drunken rabble on their way to bed, and an irate French officer telling them all to desist, as he was trying to get some sleep.

One afternoon, after his customary light breakfast, Descartes decided to take a constitutional stroll through the streets of Breda. Here he noticed a poster being stuck up on a wall. In the manner of the time, this outlined an unsolved mathematical problem, challenging all comers to try and solve it. Descartes didn't quite understand the instructions (they were, after all, in Dutch). He turned to the Dutch gentleman standing beside him, and asked if he could kindly translate. The Dutchman was unimpressed by this ignorant young French officer. He said that he was only willing to translate the poster if the Frenchman was willing to make an effort to solve the problem – and bring him his solution. The following afternoon the young French officer arrived at the Dutchman's house, where to the Dutchman's surprise he found that the French officer had not only solved the problem, but had done so in an extremely brilliant fashion.

According to Descartes' first biographer Adrien Baillet, this was how Descartes met Isaac Beekman, the renowned Dutch philosopher and mathematician. The two were to remain close friends, corresponding regularly for the next two decades (with a couple of brief interruptions owing to a clash of mathematical temperament). 'I was asleep until you wakened me,' Descartes was to write to Beekman. It was he who revived Descartes' interest in mathematics and philosophy, which had lain dormant since he had left la Flèche.

After a year or so in the Dutch army, Descartes set off on a summer tour of Germany and the Baltic. He then decided to try another spell of army life, and journeyed to the small town of Neuburg in southern Germany, where the army of Maximilian Duke of Bavaria was camped in its winter quarters on the upper reaches of the Danube. Army life here appears to have been as strenuous as ever for Descartes – who describes how he took up residence in fine warm quarters, persisted in his habit of sleeping ten hours a night and rising at noon, and spent his waking hours 'communing with my own thoughts'.

The situation in Europe was now becoming serious, though it's difficult to deduce this from Descartes' attitude. The Bavarians had gone to war against Frederick V, the Elector Palatine and Protestant King of Bohemia. The entire continent was rapidly sliding into the long and disastrous conflict which came to be known as the Thirty Years War. This war, with its ever-changing fortunes affecting countries from Sweden to Italy, was to continue until virtually the end of Descartes' life, leaving large areas of Europe, especially in Germany, devastated and deserted. Yet the effect of this war on Descartes, even when he was in the army, appears to have been minimal. However, one can't help suspecting that this persistent background of political uncertainty, together with Descartes' own psychological uncertainties, must in some way have contributed to the deep internal need for certainty which was to characterize his entire philosophy.

Meanwhile the Bavarian winter set in, and soon the snow lay round about, deep and crisp and even. Descartes found it so cold that he took to living in a stove. This is generally taken to mean a small room heated by a central stove, as is often found in Bavaria. However, Descartes does actually describe himself as living '*dans un poêle*', which incontrovertibly means 'in a stove'.

One day whilst Descartes was sitting in his stove he had a vision. It's not clear precisely what he saw, but it seems that this vision contained a mathematical picture of the world. This convinced Descartes that the workings of the entire universe could be discovered by the application of a universal mathematical science. That night when Descartes went to bed he had three vivid dreams. In the first, he found himself struggling against an overpowering wind, trying to make his way down the street towards the church at his old college in la Flèche. At one point he turns to greet someone, and the wind flings him against the church wall. Then, from the middle of the courtyard, someone calls to him that a friend of his has a melon which he wants to give him. In the next dream Descartes is overcome with terror and hears 'a noise like a crack of lightning', after which the darkness of his room is filled with a myriad of sparks. The last dream is less clear: in the course of this he sees a dictionary and a book of poetry on his desk; this is followed by a number of the usual inconsequential and highly symbolic happenings which never fail to delight the dreamer and bore everyone else. Descartes then decides (in his dream) to interpret these happenings. This might have given us a deep insight into Descartes' understanding of himself, but unfortunately his biographer Baillet becomes rather garbled at this point.

The events of that winter day and the

following night (11 November 1619) were to have a profound and lasting effect upon Descartes. He believed that this vision and the ensuing dreams had revealed to him his God-given vocation. They were to give Descartes a much-needed confidence in his calling, as well as a confidence in the correctness of its findings that was not always backed by argument. But for this experience, the brilliant dilettante might never have realized his vocation. It is ironic that Descartes, the great rationalist, should have found his inspiration in a mystical vision and some highly irrational dreams – and this element in Descartes' thinking is often overlooked in French lycées, where the great Gallic hero and hypnophile is held up as a rationalist exemplar.

Needless to say, Descartes' dreams have attracted a wide variety of explanations. According to the Dutch philosopher and astronomer Huygens, who was later to correspond with Descartes, these dreams were the result of Descartes' brain becoming overheated whilst he was in the stove. Others have suggested indigestion, overwork, lack of sleep [*sic*], a mystical crisis, or the fact that he might recently have joined the Rosicrucians. The melon, whose offstage existence is alluded to in the first dream, apparently caused much mirth to eighteenth-century readers of Descartes' biography. But with the advent of the psychoanalytic era, this melon became a much more serious matter. I see no point in going into Canteloupian detail on this point – suffice it to say that according to one commentator Freud gave 'a quite gratuitous interpretation of the melon'.

As a result of his vision and the ensuing dreams, Descartes vowed that from now on he would dedicate his life to his intellectual studies, and also make a pilgrimage of thanksgiving to the shrine of Our Lady of Loreto in Italy. So it comes as rather a surprise when we learn that Descartes continued drifting aimlessly about Europe for another five years before he made it to Loreto, and yet another two before he got down to work.

We have few precise details about Descartes during this seven-year period of 'vagabond life', as he called it. To begin with he probably joined the Imperial Hungarian army. But the Thirty Years War had now begun in earnest, and gentleman-officer Descartes appears to have been none too keen on active campaigning. After leaving the army he is known to have travelled through France, Italy, Germany, Holland, Denmark and Poland – all the time skilfully circumnavigating the regions where the Thirty Years War was being conducted by more dedicated members of his profession. Not that Descartes was able to avoid violence altogether. Whilst visiting one of the Frisian islands (possibly Schiermonnikoog), he hired a boat to take him to the mainland. The sailors mistook him for a rich French merchant, and planned to rob him. As Descartes stood on deck watching the low island shore-line recede across the grey sea, the sailors working the ropes plotted amongst themselves in Dutch. They hatched a scheme to hit him on the head, toss him overboard, and ransack the gold which they felt sure was hidden in his trunk. Unfortunately for them, their pass-enger had by now picked up a smattering of Dutch during his travels. The hapless Schier-monnikoogers found themselves confronted by dashing gentleman-officer Descartes brandishing his sword, and quickly backed down.

Some time during this period, probably in 1623, Descartes returned home to la Haye and sold all his property. The bonds he bought with the proceeds were to provide him with a good income for the rest of his life. One would think that during the course of this trip he might have called in to see his family – but this is far from certain. Descartes never actually quarrelled with his family, but he remained utterly detached from them. Despite his freedom to roam Europe at will, he didn't bother to return home for the weddings of his brother or his sister, and he didn't even visit his father on his deathbed.

Towards the end of this period Descartes spent an increasing amount of time in Paris. Here he met up with an old school friend from la Flèche, Marin Mersenne, who had joined the Church. Father Mersenne had become a highly respected man of learning, in contact with the finest mathematical and philosophical minds throughout Europe. From his cell in Paris Mersenne corresponded with such figures as Pascal, Fermat and Gassendi. Mersenne's cell became a sort of clearing house for the latest ideas current in mathematical, scientific and philosophic thinking. This was just the kind of friend Descartes needed, and he was to correspond with Mersenne for the rest of his life, sending him manuscripts and testing out his ideas on him – both for their

validity and to determine whether they con-
flicted with the teachings of the Church.

Descartes spent most of his time in Paris
closeted in his room studying, but occasionally friends would come round to discuss ideas
with him, and sometimes he was even persuaded out to more formal occasions. An
anecdote relates how Descartes was present
at the residence of the Papal Nuncio when a
certain physician called Chandoux delivered
a talk outlining his 'new philosophy'. At the
end of the talk Descartes proceeded to dis-
member this new philosophy with the aid of
some rigorous mathematical reasoning, to
which Chandoux had no reply. (Chandoux
was to find himself in a similar situation three
years later, when he was forced to defend himself against a charge of counterfeiting something more tangible than philosophical ideas,
and ended up on the gallows.) After following
Descartes' skilful arguments, Cardinal de
Bérulle took him aside and strongly advised

him to devote his entire life to philosophy.

For some reason, this appeared to do the trick. Visions and dreams may have inspired confidence in Descartes, but it took the rational approach to make him take decisive action. In 1628 Descartes retired to the north of France to live in seclusion and devote himself entirely to his thinking. But unfortunately his Parisian friends kept coming out to visit him. So Descartes journeyed even further afield, and went to live in isolation in Holland. He was to settle here for over two decades, until the year before his death.

But 'settle' is very much a relative term where Descartes is concerned. During the first fifteen years of his residence in Holland he is known to have changed house at least eighteen times – and even then, when the settled domestic routine became all too much for him, he would frequently take a trip abroad. Only Father Mersenne could keep up with his address, but at least his isolation was assured.

All this constant movement is put down to Descartes' love of solitude, but it seems to speak of some deeper restlessness. In the course of travelling, or even moving house, one can't help meeting people – even if only in superficial passing fashion. This unending movement suggests that Descartes' solitude was not entirely self-sufficient. He was lonely, but found it impossible to make contact with people except in the most trivial manner.

Descartes always had servants, and he appears to have cut quite a personable figure. The portraits we have of him depict a pale-faced gentleman in the dark flowing wig of the period, and his moustachioed drip-bearded features have a certain saturnine charm. He is said to have dressed well in fashionable knee breeches, black silk stockings and silver buckle shoes. At all times he was in the habit of wearing a silk scarf around his neck to protect it from the cold. Whenever he went out he wore a heavy coat with a woollen scarf, and always put on his sword. He is said to have been susceptible to the slightest change of temperature, which he claimed affected the 'inherited weakness' of his chest. Yet he spent years travelling all over Europe, from Italy to Scandinavia. And the country he finally chose to live in was Holland – notorious for its rain, fogs and ice, which a contemporary French visitor described as 'four months of winter followed by eight months of cold'.

Yet Holland had one great advantage. In the seventeenth century this was the duty-free zone of the European mind. Unlike other nations, here you didn't have to pay for your ideas. The tolerant Dutch had dispensed with such heavy-duty items as the Inquisition, heresy, the rack and burning at the stake – critical accolades which greeted original thinkers elsewhere in Europe. Of the four great thinkers who produced original philosophy during the seventeenth century, no fewer

than three – Descartes, Spinoza and Locke –
lived for periods in Holland. (The other, Leibnitz, lived across the border in Hanover, and
visited Holland several times.) Partly as a
result of this liberal atmosphere, Holland also
became a thriving centre of the printing indus-
try, with works by such advanced thinkers
as Galileo and Hobbes being published here.
During this period new ideas thrived in Holland as nowhere else in Europe.

Descartes started out on this productive
period of his life with high hopes. As a result
of his vision in the Bavarian stove he had conceived of a universal science capable of
embracing all human knowledge. This would
arrive at the truth by the use of reason. But
this was much more than just a revolutionary
new method. (Reason had played very much
a back-seat role in the sciences and alchemies
of the Middle Ages.) Descartes had conceived
of a system which would not only include all
knowledge, but also unite it. This system

would be free of all prejudices and assumptions, and would be based on certainty alone. It would start from basic principles, which were themselves self-evident, and would build up from these.

Descartes foresaw immense advantages resulting from his system. He confidently predicted that when this new scientific method was applied to medicine it would be able to slow down the ageing process. (This was a persistent dream of Descartes'. Ten years later he was to write to the Dutch scholar Huygens that – despite his parlous physical condition – he expected to live until he was well over a hundred. Though in the last decade of his life he revised this estimate down by a few years.)

Descartes began writing a treatise on Rules for the Direction of the Mind. In order to discover the universal science, we first had to adopt a method of thinking properly. This method consisted of following two rules of mental operation: intuition and deduction. Intuition, he defined as: 'the conception, without doubt, of an unclouded and attentive mind, which is formed by the light of reason alone'. And deduction was defined as: 'necessary inference from other facts which are known for certain'. Descartes' celebrated method – which came to be known as the Cartesian Method – lay in the correct application of these two rules of thought.

Descartes was now gaining a reputation as a thinker on a wide range of philosophical and scientific subjects. In March 1629 the Pope and certain senior cardinals began observing UFOs in the sky above Rome. As the sun set, a solar halo would appear with orbiting spots of brilliant light. Letters were sent to Descartes and various other leading thinkers, asking their opinion of these visions.

Descartes was so intrigued that for a while he gave up all philosophical thinking to concentrate on this matter. He had his suspicions about the cause of such phenomena, but refused to commit himself until several years later. By this time he had completed an entire treatise on the subject. (Meanwhile, one Vatican source had come up with its own explanation: these phenomena were caused by angels undertaking celestial scene-changes in preparation for the Second Coming.) Descartes suggested that these lights in the sky were caused by meteors. Unfortunately modern scientists have come up with an explanation which sounds even more implausible than the Vatican's. These phenomena, now called parhelia, are said to be caused when the sun shines 'through a thin cloud composed of hexagonal ice crystals falling with their principal axes vertical'. Crystals performing formation dances in the atmosphere are now considered much more likely than angels, and simplistic explanations such as Descartes' are laughed out of court.

In this, as in many other matters, Descartes

was alive during a brief and possibly unique era of human thought. The new explanations put forward by the finest scientific and philosophical minds of this period were in many cases both plausible and comprehensible. They also tended to be rational, and their overall conception to be simple – with the aim of leaving space for the contemplation of ultimate mysteries. Humanity is unlikely to experience such an era again. From then on it would become increasingly impossible to understand the truth except in the increasingly limited field of understanding which one was capable of understanding. From now on we were to know more and more about less and less.

Having laid down his rules for the working of the mind, Descartes now set about the outer world. For the next three years he composed a *Treatise on the Universe*. This contained his ideas on a huge range of scientific subjects, including meteors, dioptrics and geometry. In order to pursue his studies in anatomy he now took to visiting the local slaughterhouse, and would return home with various specimens hidden under his cloak so that he could dissect them in private. As a result of this work, Descartes originated the study of embryology. (According to legend, on one of these visits to the abattoir Descartes noticed a portly young man sketching the flayed carcase of an ox, and asked him why he had chosen such a subject. 'Your philosophy takes away our souls,' replied the artist. 'In my paintings I will give them back, even to dead animals.' The young artist is said to have been Rembrandt.)

After three long years of concentrated work Descartes prepared to send the manuscript of his *Treatise on the Universe* to Father Mersenne, so that he could have it published in Paris. Then, like a bolt from the blue, more fantastic news came through from Rome. Galileo had been charged with heresy, brought before the Inquisition, and forced to swear that he 'abjured, cursed and detested' his scientific works. Most specifically this referred to his belief in Copernicus' theory that the earth moved around the sun. Descartes immediately asked his friend Beekman for a copy of Galileo's work, and found to his dismay that many of the conclusions reached by Galileo were the same as his own. Without a word to anyone Descartes put away his *Treatise on the Universe*, and turned his thoughts to less controversial matters. (This work was not published until years after Descartes' death, and then only in part.)

Descartes' life was riven by dichotomies. He longed for peace and solitude, yet his loneliness drove him to obsessive travel. As a daringly original thinker he vowed to 'follow my thoughts wherever they might lead'; yet as a man he swore 'to obey the laws of my country, adhere to the religion of my fathers, and follow the example of the wisest men I meet'. He was convinced that what he had written in his *Treatise on the Universe* was correct, yet he also firmly believed in the God of the Church. Descartes has been accused of cowardice, of being a secret atheist, and of not even knowing himself despite all his introspective meditations. None of these accusations stands. Descartes may not have been of the stuff of martyrs, but that doesn't make him a coward. He was convinced that without dropping any of its Scholastic tenets the Church could still come round to his point of view. And his intellectual self-knowledge was deeper than that of any philosopher since Socrates, even if it did contain a few psychological blind spots.

Yet the greatest dichotomy which beset Descartes lay in his philosophy. Descartes saw the world as consisting of two kinds of substance – mind and matter. Mind was unextended and indivisible. Matter was extended and divisible, and obeyed the laws of physics. This meant that our incorporeal mind was lodged in a mechanistic body. But how could the mind, which had no extension, interact with a body which could only obey the mechanistic laws of science? Descartes never satisfactorily solved this problem – which so uncannily echoes the psychological dichotomies that beset him in daily life. Yet, as ever, he did try to come up with an answer. According to Descartes, the mind and the body interact in the pineal gland (an obscure organ near the base of the brain, whose precise function remains uncertain to this day). Unfortunately, Descartes rather missed the point here. The question was not so much where they interact, but how.

At this stage a rare human element enters Descartes' life. He has an affair with a girl called Hélène, who may possibly have been one of his servants. As a result he has a daughter, whom he calls Francine. After the birth of Francine, Hélène lives with her daughter in a nearby house, but visits him regularly. When others are present, Descartes passes off Francine as his niece.

From these few facts it's difficult to know for certain what kind of relationship he had with Hélène. But it's easy enough to conjecture. Poor Hélène – what did she make of this upper-class cold fish? What did she register when she gazed into those shadow-ringed abstracted eyes of his? . . . Hélène may not have been able to break through to Descartes, but Francine certainly did. Guilelessly she reached out to him, and he responded. (It wasn't so much that he'd been rejected in his childhood: there was just no one there, except old nanny with her potato love.) Despite attempting to pass Francine off as his niece, Descartes soon grew to love his little daughter. This was a unique emotional experience in his life.

Descartes was now writing what is today considered as his most original work, his *Discourse on Method*. Ironically, the body of this book consisted of safer bits lifted from his *Treatise on the Universe*. These contained ideas which were to change the face of mathematics and make several revolutionary advances in science. In this work Descartes laid the foundations of modern analytic geometry and introduced co-ordinates (later to be named Cartesian co-ordinates, by Leibnitz); in optics he proposed the Law of Diffraction, and put forward an explanation of the rainbow; and he also attempted a rational scientific theory to explain the weather (which, like modern meteorological theories, is only defeated by the ultimate irrationality of this phenomenon).

Yet by far and away the best part of the *Discourse on Method* is the comparatively brief introduction. This outlines the essential ideas in his thinking that were to change the course of philosophy. And in an even more revolutionary departure from tradition, Descartes makes these ideas both comprehensible and readable.

How is it possible to convey your profoundly original philosophical insights with sufficient clarity so that anyone else can actually understand them? This problem has not only defeated you and me, but also most of the great minds of philosophy. Plato cracked it by setting out his philosophy in the form of dinner party conversations. Nietzsche thought he'd cracked it by writing the most brilliant, subtle and powerful prose ever penned in German, but this megalomania turned into pure mania. Wittgenstein attempted to circumvent the problem by allowing for the attention span of the TV age and writing brilliant two-line remarks, but this left no room to back them up with philosophic argument. Descartes succeeded in overcoming this problem by the simplest and most obvious method of all. In clear autobiographical prose he describes how he goes about his thinking, and the thoughts which occur to him in the process. When you read Descartes you experience what it is like to be a great mind thinking original philosophy.

And he describes this so deceptively well that you think it's easy – it appears no different from the way you might think. Step by rational step you follow him to his conclusion.

Descartes begins by taking us back to snow-covered Bavaria and the time of his vision. 'Winter set in, and I found myself in a spot where there was no society of any interest. At the time I was unworried by any cares or passions, so I took to spending my day in a stove, where I could be alone with my thoughts.' In surprisingly cool prose he then goes on to describe how it is possible, by means of persistent and determined doubt, for us to destroy our belief in the entire fabric of the world around us. Nothing remains certain. The whole universe, our very individuality, even our own existence, could all be a dream. We have no way of knowing anything for certain. Except for one thing. No matter how deluded I may be in my thoughts about myself and the world, there is just one thing that is undeniable. I am thinking. This alone proves to me my existence. In the most famous remark in philosophy, Descartes concludes: 'Cogito ergo sum.' (I think therefore I am.)

Having established his one ultimate certainty, Descartes proceeds to rebuild upon this foundation all that he has doubted. The world, the truths of mathematics, the snowbound Bavarian winter – all return with cold certainty, chastened by their period of banishment to the never-never land of doubt, but more indubitable than ever now that they are built on such an indubitable foundation.

Having had the courage to doubt the entire universe, Descartes typically chose to publish this work anonymously. He also published it in French, in the hope of reaching a wider audience. He wished to avoid controversy with the Church, and hoped to do so by appealing to people who were interested in the new sciences. Astonishingly, this almost worked. Almost. People soon recognized who was the author of *Discourse on Method*, but to begin with they were more interested in its mathematical and scientific theories. The mathematicians were at first fascinated, and then outraged.

For most of us the one certain thing about mathematics is that it's either correct or incorrect. Such a naïve approach immediately disqualifies one from the realm of true mathematicians. Here at the genius level the puerile objectivity of right and wrong gives way to a more knowledgeable combative approach. Aggression increases (by geometric progression) the more it encounters the incontrovertible. Having read Descartes' new mathematical theories, and recognized their profound originality, all the great mathematicians of the era were soon gunning for Descartes. Gassendi, Pascal, Insen, Fermat . . . one by one they entered the fray.

Such controversies are well beyond the comprehension of mere mortals. Those who believe otherwise might find the old story of Fermat's Last Theorem instructive. According to this, there are no whole numbers above one, such that the following expression is true:

$$X^n + Y^n = Z^n$$

Shortly before Fermat died he wrote in the margin beside this formula: 'I have discovered a truly remarkable proof for this, but there's no room to write it down here.' Despite repeated attempts by many of the finest mathematical minds of the past three centuries, no one has yet managed either to prove or disprove Fermat's Last Theorem. Some say that it can't possibly be true. Others that it must be. Some are convinced that Fermat was bluffing, still others that he didn't dare to try and prove it . . . Mathematics begins in certainty, and ends like this. Philosophy, on the other hand, both begins and ends like this. When someone is described as having a philosophical attitude, you can be sure he's not a philosopher. This Descartes quickly discovered. After the mathematicians, it was the philosophers' turn to launch into the fray. In no time Descartes found himself in hot water with the Church. If you could doubt everything except the fact that you were thinking, where did this leave God? Descartes was very lucky not to find himself in something hotter than water. But fortunately his friends rallied round to defend him – and even more fortunately Descartes was living in Holland.

Or rather, moving in Holland. In 1638, for the fifteenth time since taking up residence in the United Provinces of the Netherlands, Descartes moved house once again – this time to Amersfoot, just outside the ancient university city of Utrecht. By now his daughter Francine was five years old, and he was planning to send her to France so that she could become 'a fine lady'. Then suddenly Francine took ill and died. Descartes was devastated. This was the most bitter blow he was to suffer during his entire life, and according to his biographer Baillet 'he wept for his child with a tenderness which showed that the thought of eternity is capable of being extinguished by the grief of the moment'.

This tragedy occurred whilst Descartes was putting the finishing touches to his *Meditations*. This work is generally considered as his masterpiece. Though not as immediately appealing as the *Discourse on Method*, it is graced with the same felicity of style and its French is a model expression of abstract thought. (Descartes gallantly claimed that he had written it with the aim of making abstract ideas exciting to women.) But this time he took the precaution of sending the manuscript to Father Mersenne in Paris, and asking him to distribute it so that he might discover 'the opinions of the learned'. Descartes wished to have the approval of the scholars and the Jesuits for his new philosophical treatise –

which contained an elaboration of the ideas put forward in the *Discourse on Method*. This time he proposes an even more comprehensive programme of doubt. He imagines that the entire universe, even the truths of geometry and the winter dressing-gown he is wearing as he sits in front of the fire, may be the work of a malignant unseen being intent on deceiving him. (Psychologists have confidently identified the anti-hero of this fantasy as Judge Joachim Descartes.) Once again the doubtful workings of Descartes' mind arrive at the same indisputable cog. And upon this self-evident principle of ultimate certainty he once again rebuilds the universe. He even goes so far as to prove the existence of God – with arguments first used by Sts Anselm and Thomas Aquinas over four centuries earlier – presumably in order to make the Church feel more at home.

Although this process of Cartesian doubt was not strictly speaking original, it was considered as such at the time. St Augustine's remarkably similar doubts and conclusion, put forward twelve centuries previously, were not central to his thought and had been completely ignored. But nearer to Descartes' own times, and more interestingly, the Portuguese philosopher Francisco Sanches had proposed almost exactly the same programme of comprehensive doubt in his astonishing treatise *Quod Nihil Scitur* (Why nothing can be known). This had been published in 1581. Fortunately for Sanches his treatise attracted little attention, or he might have ended up as a great philosophic martyr at the age of thirty-one, rather than dying in comfortable obscurity in Toulouse at the ripe old age of seventy-three.

Descartes had no ambitions for martyrdom, and though he possessed many of the qualifications for obscurity (under other circumstances, his sloth alone would surely have qualified him) he appears to have had no ambitions in this direction either. Descartes wanted to be heard, but he also wanted to be accepted. He was utterly convinced that he was right, but he wanted the Church to be convinced too. So under Descartes' instructions Father Mersenne sent out the manuscript of the *Meditations* to such luminaries of the European intellectual scene as Gassendi, Hobbes and Arnauld. And they replied, putting forward their objections to Descartes' theories. These objections irritated Descartes, but he was persuaded to add his replies – and the *Meditations* were finally published, complete with objections, and Descartes' rebuttals of these objections.

Inevitably, the publication of Descartes' *Meditations* resulted in an even worse furore. The Jesuits correctly realized that Cartesian doubt and *Cogito ergo sum* spelled the end of Scholastic philosophy and Aquinas. But worse still for Descartes, this time the controversy spilled over into Holland. The president of the University of Utrecht accused Descartes of

atheism. Ingeniously, he likened Descartes to
Vanini, who had been charged with purposely
putting forward weak and ineffectual proofs
of the existence of God. (Vanini had been
burned at the stake in 1619, in Toulouse –
watched perhaps from the edge of the crowd by
an obscure old Portuguese professor muttering
to himself, 'There but for the grace of God . . .')
The attack on Descartes by the president of the
University of Utrecht was followed by some
even more damaging attacks from other impor-
tant Dutch figures, accusing him of heresy. In
those days atheism was one thing, but heresy
was a *really* serious matter. Fortunately the
French ambassador intervened on Descartes'
behalf, and eventually the matter blew over,
though for some time afterwards Descartes'
name and works were not allowed to be men-
tioned, either favourably or unfavourably,
within the precincts of the University of
Utrecht. But this ban was eventually dropped,
after the mathematics department complained

that they were unable to do any geometry.

Descartes was now renowned throughout Europe, his fame stretching so far beyond the intellectual world that he was even read by royalty. When the young Queen Christina of Sweden read one of his books she was so impressed that she decided to invite him to court. Descartes must come to Stockholm and teach her philosophy. By now the long hard years of late rising and gentlemanly meditation were beginning to take their toll on Descartes. Although he was only fifty-three, he hadn't moved house for four years. Descartes was at this stage living on a small estate at Egmond-Binnen, twenty miles north of Amsterdam near the sea. He did his meditations sitting in his octagonal study looking out over a beautiful old garden. Occasionally he would take a trip to Paris, where he discussed his ideas with old sparring partners such as Gassendi, Pascal, Hobbes and Arnauld.

The prospect of a long trip north to 'the

land of bears between rock and ice' (as he called Sweden) did not appeal. But Queen Christina was a headstrong and determined woman. Only twenty-three years old, she had already made her mark on her kingdom. Just five foot tall, she had broad shoulders and trained like a soldier. It was said that she could gallop for over ten hours without tiring (though one wonders about the horse). When she ascended the throne she vowed to turn her capital, the watery Venice of the North, into the intellectual Paris of the North. Yet despite her determined efforts, it still remained undeniably the Stockholm of the North. Descartes was her big chance, and she was determined not to let him slip from her grasp. To reinforce her invitation she sent over an admiral and a warship to collect him. But Descartes cavilled, albeit in most gallant fashion, handing to the waiting admiral a flattering missive describing how 'Her Majesty was created in the image of God to a greater degree than the rest of mankind', but prayed to be excused from 'basking in the sunbeams of her glorious presence'.

Christina stamped her foot, the court had a bad day, she galloped on her horse for hours on end – and another ship of the line was despatched to Holland. Descartes, who had defeated the finest minds of Europe in intellectual argument, was eventually forced to concede defeat. He sailed for Stockholm in October 1649, where he was given a five-star welcoming ceremony by Queen Christina. There followed two personal audiences with Her Majesty, who appeared to have absorbed little philosophy from the study of his works; and then the Queen decided there were other matters requiring her attention. Descartes was left kicking his heels for six weeks, while the bitter Swedish winter set in. It was to be the worst for sixty years: the city icebound for six months, gloom at noon, and beyond the suburbs the wolves howling in the frigid blast beneath the Aurora Borealis.

Mindful of the great mind going to waste in her capital, Christina commissioned a brand new work from Descartes. Reluctantly the philosopher set about composing verses to be set to music for a ballet called 'The Birth of Peace', which Christina wanted performed on her birthday. Descartes must have been pretty good at musicals, because as soon as he'd finished this one he was put to work writing a musical comedy about two princes who were under the impression that they were shepherds. (Unfortunately, I could find no reference to these in Descartes' collected works – only Descartes' glum comment: 'men's thoughts freeze here during winter months'.)

Then midway through January, Christina decided that it was time she started her philosophy lessons. Descartes was duly summoned, and informed that the Queen would have three philosophy lessons a week, each starting at five a.m.

Even in the army Descartes had never risen

before eleven a.m. The shock of rising at four a.m. in deepest Scandinavian winter, attending to his toilet with French fastidiousness during the Hour of the Wolf – followed by a fast bumpy sleigh-ride over the iron-iced streets through the piercing Arctic blast ... No, there's no point in even trying to imagine how Descartes felt. Within two weeks he caught a chill, which soon turned into pneumonia. A week later he became delirious, and he died on 11 February 1650. One of Europe's greatest intellectuals had been sacrificed to the whim of royalty. As a Catholic, in Protestant Sweden, this deeply religious man could not be buried in sacred ground – but had to be interred in the cemetery for unbaptized children.

Thirteen years after his death the Catholic Church honoured Descartes' memory by placing all his works on its Index of banned books (thus ensuring that they would continue to be read for years to come). Later in the seven-

teenth century Descartes' body was trans-
ferred to Paris where it was reinterred. During
the Revolution it was proposed that he should
be exhumed again and placed in the Pantheon,
alongside other great French thinkers. This
was put to the National Assembly. In an
unusual move, the members divided along
scientific lines. Those who favoured the mechanistic Cartesian view of the universe were
opposed by members who supported the new
Newtonian theory of gravity. Descartes had
proposed the Theory of Vortices to explain
how the universe worked. His theory maintained that the movement of one particle
effected the movement of all other particles
throughout the universe. This took place
through a series of interlocking vortices –
which encompassed everything from the solar
system and the stars down to the smallest particles. (This would of course have resulted in
a system of fiendish complexity, such as only
a mathematician could conceive. Yet it points

to a matter of some interest in the evolution of human thought. Descartes' theory bears a passing resemblance both to the double helix of DNA and the Superstring Theory of ultimate particles. Also, in his long search for a force that could interact between mind and body, Descartes was looking for something similar to radio waves or electricity. According to the modern thinker Jean de Mandeville, this points to the possibility that human understanding evolves along certain conceptual lines almost regardless of its object.)

When it came to the vote in the French National Assembly, the Newtonians managed to muster sufficient support to defeat the Cartesians. Gravity had won the day. Descartes would have to be buried elsewhere.

Formerly the truth had been the province of theology, now it had entered the realm of democracy. Descartes didn't fit into either. Appropriately, he is now buried in the Church of St Germain des Prés, in the heart of the

Latin Quarter in Paris, where his tradition of doubtful thinking and noon rising is staunchly maintained to this day.

Afterword

Prior to Descartes, philosophy had fallen asleep. The modern age of philosophy begins with Descartes. From this period, the primacy of the individual and the analysis of human consciousness became fundamental to philosophy. In one form or another, this has remained so until comparatively recently. Only with the arrival of logical analysis was the primacy of the individual and analysis of human consciousness superseded by the primacy of the dictionary and analysis of its contents. Once more, philosophy stands in need of a Descartes to wake it up.

Key quotations

It is some time since I first realized how many false opinions I accepted as true from my childhood, and how doubtful was the entire structure of thought which I had built upon them. I therefore understood that I must, if I wanted to establish anything at all in science that was firm and liable to last, once and for all rid myself of all the opinions I had adopted, and start from an entirely new foundation.

Meditations, I: opening lines.

A multitude of laws often hampers justice, so that a state is best governed when it has only a few laws which are strictly administered; similarly, instead of the large number of laws which make up logic, I was of the opinion that the four following laws were perfectly sufficient for me, provided I took the firm and unwavering resolution to stick to them clearly at all times.

The first was never to accept anything as true if I did not clearly know it to be so; that is, carefully to avoid precipitate conclusions and preconceptions, and to include nothing more in my judgement than was presented clearly and distinctly to my mind so that I had no reason to doubt it.

The second, to divide each of the difficulties I examined into as many parts as possible, and as might be necessary for a proper solution.

The third, to conduct my thoughts in an orderly fashion, by starting with the simplest and most easily known objects, so that I could ascend, little by little, and step by step, to more complex knowledge; and by giving some order even to those objects which appeared to have none.

And the last, always to make enumerations so complete, and reviews so comprehensive, that I could be sure of leaving nothing out.

Discourse on Method, part I

The long chains of simple and easy reasonings, which geometers use to reach the most difficult conclusions, had given me reason to suppose that all things which can be known by humanity are connected in some way. And that there is nothing so far removed from us as to be beyond our reach, or so hidden that we cannot discover it, as long as we abstain from accepting the false for the true, and always preserve in our thoughts the order necessary for the deduction of one truth from another. Also, I had little difficulty in determining the objects with which it was necessary to commence, for I was already convinced that these must be the simplest and easiest known.

Discourse on Method, part II

Since I desired to devote myself wholly to the search for truth, I thought it necessary . . . to reject as if utterly false anything in which I could discover the least grounds for doubt, so that I could find out if I was left with anything at all which was absolutely indubitable. Thus, because our senses sometimes deceive us, I decided to suppose that nothing was really as they led us to believe it was. And, because some of us make mistakes in reasoning, committing logical errors in even the simplest matters of geometry, I rejected as erroneous all reasonings that I had previously taken as proofs. And finally, when I considered that the very same things we perceive when we are awake, may also occur to us while we are asleep and not perceiving anything at all, I resolved to pretend that anything which had ever entered my mind was no more than a dream. But immediately I noticed that while I was thinking in this way, and regarding everything as false, it was nonetheless absolutely necessary that I, who was doing this thinking, was still something. And observing that this truth 'I think, therefore I am' was so sure and certain that no ground for doubt, be it ever so extravagantly sceptical, was capable of shaking it, I therefore decided that I could accept it without scruple as the first principle of the philosophy I was seeking to create.

Discourse on Method, part IV

There is a vast difference between the mind and the body, in that the body by its very nature is always divisible, whilst the mind is completely indivisible. For when I consider the mind, or rather when I consider myself simply as a thinking thing, I find I can distinguish no parts within myself, and I clearly discern that I am a thing utterly one and complete. Although my whole mind seems to be united to my whole body, when a foot, or an arm, or any other part is severed, I am not conscious of anything having been removed from my mind. Nor can the faculties of willing, perceiving, conceptualizing and so forth, in any way be called parts of the mind, as it is always the same mind which is doing the willing, perceiving, conceptualizing and so forth. Meanwhile, utterly the opposite holds for all corporeal or extended things. For I cannot imagine any one of them which I cannot in my thoughts easily split into parts, and thus I understand that it is divisible.

Meditations, 6

Good sense is most evenly distributed amongst all humanity; for all consider themselves to be so well endowed with it that even those who complain of their lot in all other ways seldom express the desire for more good sense. And here it is unlikely that everyone is mistaken. It shows rather that the power of correct judgement and the ability to distinguish truth from error – what we properly call good sense or reason – is by nature equally given to all humanity. As a result, the diversity of our opinions does not arise from any of us being endowed with a greater quantity of reason, but solely because we direct our thoughts in different directions and do not pay attention to the same things. For it is not enough just to have a fine mind; the main thing is to learn how to apply it properly. The finest minds are capable of both the greatest vices as well as the greatest virtues; and those who travel slowly often make better progress, as long as they follow the right path, than those who rush ahead and stray from it.

Discourse on Method, part I

Chronology of significant philosophical dates

6th century BC	The start of western philosophy with Thales of Miletus.
end of 6th century BC	Death of Pythagoras.
399 BC	Socrates sentenced to death in Athens.
c387 BC	Plato founds the Academy in Athens, the first university.
335 BC	Aristotle founds the Lyceum in Athens, rival school to the Academy.
324 AD	Emperor Constantine moves capital of Roman Empire to Byzantium.
400 AD	St Augustine writes his

	Confessions. Philosophy absorbed into Christian theology.
410 AD	Sack of Rome by Visigoths.
529 AD	Closure of Academy in Athens by Emperor Justinian marks end of Greco-Roman era and start of Dark Ages.
mid 13th Century	Thomas Aquinas writes his commentaries on Aristotle. Era of Scholasticism.
1453	Fall of Byzantium to Turks, end of Byzantine Empire.
1492	Columbus reaches America. Renaissance in Florence and revival of interest in Greek learning.
1543	Copernicus publishes *De revolutionibus orbium caelestium* (*On the Revolution of the Celestial Orbs*) proving

mathematically that the earth revolves around the sun.

1633   Galileo forced by Church to recant heliocentric theory of the universe.

1641   Descartes publishes his *Meditations*, the start of modern philosophy.

1677   Death of Spinoza allows publication of his *Ethics*.

1687   Newton publishes *Principia*, introducing concept of gravity.

1689   Locke publishes *Essay Concerning Human Understanding*. Start of Empiricism.

1710   Berkeley publishes *Principles of Human Knowledge*, advancing Empiricism to new extremes.

1716   Death of Leibnitz.

1739–40   Hume publishes *Treatise of Human Nature*, taking Empiricism to its logical limits.

1781   Kant, woken from his 'dogmatic slumbers' by Hume, publishes *Critique of Pure Reason*. Great era of German metaphysics begins.

1807   Hegel publishes *The Phenomenology of Mind*: high point of German metaphysics.

1818   Schopenhauer publishes *The World as Will and Representation*, introducing Indian philosophy into German metaphysics.

1889   Nietzsche, having declared 'God is dead', succumbs to madness in Turin.

1921   Wittgenstein publishes

Tractatus-Logico-Philosophicus, claiming the 'final solution' to the problems of philosophy.

1920s   Vienna Circle propound Logical Positivism.

1927   Heidegger publishes *Sein und Zeit* (*Being and Time*), heralding split between analytical and continental philosophy.

1943   Sartre publishes *L'être et le néant* (*Being and Nothingness*), advancing Heidegger's thought and instigating Existentialism.

1953   Posthumous publication of Wittgenstein's *Philosophical Investigations*. High era of Linguistic Analysis.